Astrology for Busy Bees

Astrology for Busy Bees

Matthew Petchinsky

Astrology for Busy Bees: Star Signs Simplified
By: Matthew Petchinsky

Introduction: Unlocking the Stars for Everyday Life

Astrology, often regarded as the language of the cosmos, has fascinated humanity for millennia. It connects us to the rhythms of the universe and serves as a map to navigate the complexities of life. Yet, for many, astrology remains shrouded in mystery, or worse, misunderstood as mere superstition or fortune-telling. This book is here to change that perception. It's not about vague predictions or convoluted jargon—it's about practical, actionable tools for understanding yourself and improving your daily life.

Astrology as a Tool for Self-Discovery

At its core, astrology is a system for self-awareness. It reveals patterns in your personality, highlights your strengths, and uncovers areas for growth. By understanding these cosmic influences, you can align your choices with your natural tendencies and live a more intentional and fulfilling life. Whether you're seeking clarity in relationships, career, or personal development, astrology offers a framework to guide your decisions with confidence.

Think of astrology as a mirror that reflects who you are—not a fixed destiny but a set of potentials waiting to be realized. The stars don't dictate your future; they illuminate your path, offering insights that can empower you to navigate life's challenges and seize opportunities.

Addressing Misconceptions

One of the biggest misconceptions about astrology is that it's overly complex, reserved for those with hours to study intricate birth charts or memorize planetary placements. Others may dismiss it as pseudoscience, disconnected from reality. This book aims to dispel these myths by simplifying astrology into an approachable, time-efficient system that anyone can use.

You don't need to become an expert to benefit from astrology. You don't need to know the difference between a sextile and a quincunx (though we'll touch on that, too). Instead, you'll find bite-sized insights designed for people who have limited time but a strong desire for self-improvement.

What This Book Covers

In this book, we'll break astrology down into practical, easy-to-understand pieces, focusing on how you can apply it to your daily life. Each chapter is designed to provide quick, actionable insights that you can implement immediately. Whether you have five minutes or an entire afternoon, you'll find tools and techniques tailored to your schedule.

Here's what you can expect to learn:

- **Your Zodiac Sign and Beyond**: Understand the traits and tendencies of your Sun sign while discovering the deeper layers of your Moon and Rising signs.
- **Planetary Influences**: Learn how the positions of planets like Mercury, Venus, and Mars shape your communication style, relationships, and drive.
- **Practical Applications**: From planning your week according to the Moon's phases to leveraging Mercury retrograde for self-reflection, this book focuses on actionable advice.
- **Simplified Charts**: Explore basic techniques to read your own chart, even if you've never looked at one before.
- **Real-Life Benefits**: Use astrology to improve decision-making, build stronger relationships, and create a more aligned and fulfilling life.

This book isn't about adding more to your to-do list; it's about integrating astrology seamlessly into your existing routines.

Why Astrology Matters

In today's fast-paced world, it's easy to feel disconnected—from ourselves, from others, and from the natural cycles of life. Astrology serves as a bridge, reconnecting us to these essential rhythms. It reminds us that we are part of something larger, something meaningful, and something infinitely beautiful.

As you embark on this journey, keep an open mind and a curious heart. Astrology is not a strict doctrine but a tool—one that you can adapt to suit your unique needs and goals. Whether you're a skeptic dipping your toes into the cosmic waters or a seasoned enthusiast looking for fresh perspectives, this book is designed to inspire, educate, and empower you.

The stars are always there, offering their guidance. Are you ready to listen? Let's unlock their wisdom together.

Chapter 1: Understanding Your Sun Sign

Astrology begins with the Sun sign, the cornerstone of your astrological identity. Often referred to as your "star sign," the Sun sign is determined by the position of the Sun in the zodiac at the time of your birth. While the Sun takes center stage in most horoscopes and popular astrology, its significance runs much deeper than generic predictions. Your Sun sign represents your core self—your vitality, life force, and the essence of who you are.

The Significance of the Sun Sign

The Sun is the brightest celestial body in our solar system, symbolizing life, energy, and identity. In astrology, it governs your ego, willpower, and sense of purpose. Think of the Sun sign as your inner light—it defines what drives you, what fulfills you, and how you shine in the world. It's the unchanging essence of your personality, guiding you even as circumstances around you evolve.

The Sun sign influences your ambitions, values, and the qualities you naturally express. While your Moon sign and Rising sign add nuance to your personality, your Sun sign is the foundation. Understanding it can provide clarity about your strengths, motivations, and challenges, empowering you to navigate life with greater self-awareness.

The 12 Sun Signs and Their Defining Characteristics

Each Sun sign corresponds to a segment of the zodiac and carries unique energies and traits. Below is a quick breakdown of the 12 Sun signs, grouped by their element: Fire, Earth, Air, and Water.

Fire Signs: Bold, Passionate, and Energetic

- **Aries (March 21 - April 19)**
  Characteristics: Ambitious, adventurous, and dynamic. Aries is a natural leader with boundless energy and enthusiasm.
  Challenge: Impulsiveness and impatience.
  Strength Tip: Channel your drive into constructive goals, and practice patience with yourself and others.
- **Leo (July 23 - August 22)**
  Characteristics: Confident, charismatic, and creative. Leo thrives on recognition and has a natural flair for drama.
  Challenge: Pride and a tendency to dominate.
  Strength Tip: Use your charisma to inspire others and stay open to collaboration.
- **Sagittarius (November 22 - December 21)**
  Characteristics: Optimistic, curious, and adventurous. Sagittarius loves exploring new ideas, cultures, and experiences.
  Challenge: Restlessness and over-commitment.
  Strength Tip: Focus your energy on meaningful pursuits and allow time for reflection.

Earth Signs: Practical, Reliable, and Grounded

- **Taurus (April 20 - May 20)**
  Characteristics: Patient, determined, and sensual. Taurus values comfort, beauty, and stability.
  Challenge: Stubbornness and resistance to change.
  Strength Tip: Leverage your perseverance to achieve long-term goals, but remain flexible when needed.
- **Virgo (August 23 - September 22)**
  Characteristics: Analytical, detail-oriented, and service-driven. Virgo excels at organization and problem-solving.
  Challenge: Overthinking and perfectionism.
  Strength Tip: Trust your instincts and know when to let go of minor imperfections.
- **Capricorn (December 22 - January 19)**
  Characteristics: Ambitious, disciplined, and responsible. Capricorn is a natural planner with a strong work ethic.
  Challenge: Workaholism and rigidity.
  Strength Tip: Balance work with relaxation and celebrate your accomplishments.

Air Signs: Intellectual, Communicative, and Adaptable

- **Gemini (May 21 - June 20)**
  Characteristics: Curious, witty, and versatile. Gemini thrives on intellectual stimulation and social interaction.
  Challenge: Indecisiveness and superficiality.
  Strength Tip: Focus on deepening your commitments to a few key interests or relationships.
- **Libra (September 23 - October 22)**
  Characteristics: Diplomatic, charming, and fair-minded. Libra values harmony and beauty in all forms.
  Challenge: Avoiding conflict and people-pleasing.
  Strength Tip: Stand firm in your decisions while maintaining your natural diplomacy.
- **Aquarius (January 20 - February 18)**
  Characteristics: Innovative, independent, and visionary. Aquarius is driven by big ideas and the desire to improve the world.
  Challenge: Detachment and rebelliousness.
  Strength Tip: Balance your individuality with empathy for others' perspectives.

Water Signs: Emotional, Intuitive, and Compassionate

- **Cancer (June 21 - July 22)**
  Characteristics: Nurturing, protective, and empathetic. Cancer values home and emotional security.
  Challenge: Moodiness and over-sensitivity.
  Strength Tip: Use your intuition to build strong connections and establish healthy emotional boundaries.
- **Scorpio (October 23 - November 21)**
  Characteristics: Passionate, resourceful, and intense. Scorpio excels at transformation and uncovering hidden truths.
  Challenge: Jealousy and secrecy.
  Strength Tip: Channel your intensity into personal growth and creative expression.
- **Pisces (February 19 - March 20)**
  Characteristics: Imaginative, empathetic, and artistic. Pisces is deeply connected to dreams and the collective unconscious.
  Challenge: Escapism and indecisiveness.
  Strength Tip: Ground your creativity with practical routines and realistic goals.

Practical Tips for Leveraging Your Sun Sign Strengths

1. **Embrace Your Strengths**
   Identify the traits that make your Sun sign unique and celebrate them. Whether it's Aries' courage, Taurus' persistence, or Pisces' creativity, lean into the qualities that empower you.

2. **Navigate Your Challenges**
   Each Sun sign has its shadow side. Acknowledge these tendencies and develop strategies to manage them. For example, if you're a Capricorn prone to overwork, set aside time for self-care.

3. **Set Aligned Goals**
   Use your Sun sign's energy to guide your goals. Fire signs can channel their passion into leadership roles, while Earth signs may thrive in structured, long-term projects.

4. **Strengthen Relationships**
   Understanding your Sun sign can improve how you interact with others. Recognize how your traits influence your communication style and adapt to complement the signs of those around you.

5. **Create Daily Rituals**
   Align your daily routines with your Sun sign's energy. A Gemini might benefit from journaling to organize their thoughts, while a Cancer might find solace in creating a cozy, nurturing home environment.

Final Thoughts

Your Sun sign is the starting point for exploring astrology, offering a wealth of insight into your personality and purpose. By understanding its significance, you can harness its strengths and overcome its challenges, creating a life that reflects your true self. As you delve deeper into the chapters ahead, remember that the Sun sign is just one piece of the puzzle—but it's a brilliant place to begin.

Chapter 2: The Moon Sign: Your Emotional Compass

While your Sun sign represents your core self and ego, your Moon sign governs the unseen depths of your emotional world. It's the quiet yet powerful force that shapes your feelings, instincts, and intuition. Understanding your Moon sign offers a gateway to mastering your emotional responses, deepening your self-awareness, and nurturing your inner well-being.

What Is the Moon Sign?

The Moon sign is determined by the position of the Moon in the zodiac at the exact time of your birth. Unlike the Sun, which remains in one sign for about a month, the Moon changes signs every 2-3 days. This rapid movement gives the Moon a dynamic and deeply personal influence on your inner life.

If the Sun sign is your outward identity, the Moon sign is your inner sanctuary. It represents how you process emotions, your instinctual reactions, and what makes you feel safe and secure. It also reflects your subconscious desires and the way you care for yourself and others.

In relationships, the Moon sign plays a crucial role in compatibility, as it governs emotional needs and how you connect on a deeper level. It's also tied to intuition, revealing how you interpret subtle signals and gut feelings.

How to Identify Your Moon Sign

To discover your Moon sign, you'll need the following details:

1. **Date of Birth**: The exact date is essential since the Moon changes signs every few days.
2. **Time of Birth**: Precise timing helps pinpoint your Moon sign, especially if the Moon was transitioning between signs on your birth date.
3. **Place of Birth**: The location adjusts for time zones and influences the Moon's placement.

You can use online Moon sign calculators or an astrological charting tool to find this information. If you're unsure of your birth time, your Moon sign can still be estimated, though it may not be entirely accurate if it falls on a cusp.

The Emotional Traits of Each Moon Sign

Below is a breakdown of how each Moon sign influences emotional patterns, intuition, and self-care needs.

Fire Signs: Aries, Leo, Sagittarius

- **Aries Moon**: Emotionally intense and quick to react. Prefers direct expression of feelings and seeks independence in relationships.
  Self-Care Tip: Engage in physical activities like exercise to release pent-up energy.
- **Leo Moon**: Needs recognition and affection to feel emotionally secure. Expressive and dramatic in sharing feelings.
  Self-Care Tip: Surround yourself with people who uplift and appreciate you.
- **Sagittarius Moon**: Thrives on freedom and emotional exploration. Prefers optimism and avoids heavy emotional constraints.
  Self-Care Tip: Travel or learn something new to rejuvenate your spirit.

Earth Signs: Taurus, Virgo, Capricorn

- **Taurus Moon**: Emotionally steady and values comfort and security. Seeks stability in relationships and avoids unnecessary drama.
  Self-Care Tip: Create a soothing environment with favorite scents, foods, or cozy spaces.
- **Virgo Moon**: Analytical and practical with emotions. May overthink feelings but is deeply caring in subtle ways.
  Self-Care Tip: Practice mindfulness or journaling to release emotional clutter.

- **Capricorn Moon**: Emotionally reserved but highly dependable. Seeks achievements and practical solutions to emotional challenges.
Self-Care Tip: Set small, realistic goals to boost emotional confidence.

Air Signs: Gemini, Libra, Aquarius

- **Gemini Moon**: Quick to process emotions intellectually. Thrives on communication and often needs to talk through feelings.
Self-Care Tip: Connect with a trusted friend or write out your thoughts for clarity.
- **Libra Moon**: Emotionally balanced and values harmony in relationships. Seeks fairness and avoids conflict.
Self-Care Tip: Indulge in art or beauty to restore emotional equilibrium.
- **Aquarius Moon**: Detached and objective with emotions. Values independence and unconventional forms of emotional expression.
Self-Care Tip: Spend time brainstorming creative solutions to problems or helping others in unique ways.

Water Signs: Cancer, Scorpio, Pisces

- **Cancer Moon**: Deeply nurturing and emotionally sensitive. Needs strong connections with family or close friends for security.
Self-Care Tip: Create a safe, comforting space to retreat when overwhelmed.
- **Scorpio Moon**: Intense and transformative with emotions. Seeks depth and truth in all emotional exchanges.
Self-Care Tip: Explore your feelings through introspective practices like meditation or therapy.

- **Pisces Moon**: Imaginative and empathetic. Often absorbs the emotions of others and seeks spiritual or artistic outlets.
  Self-Care Tip: Set boundaries to protect your energy and engage in creative activities.

Using Your Moon Sign for Stress Management

Your Moon sign holds the key to understanding how you naturally handle stress and what you need to feel secure during challenging times. Here's how to leverage its insights:

- **Fire Moons**: Burn off stress through action. Physical activity or a bold creative outlet can help restore balance.
- **Earth Moons**: Turn to routines or nature. Grounding activities like gardening, cooking, or walking outdoors provide relief.
- **Air Moons**: Talk it out. Sharing your thoughts or reading something inspiring can help process stress.
- **Water Moons**: Lean into emotions. Journaling, crying, or spending time near water can be soothing.

Nurturing Relationships with Moon Sign Insights

Knowing your Moon sign can improve your relationships by helping you understand your emotional needs and those of others. Consider these strategies:

- Identify how you express emotions. Are you more reserved (Earth/Capricorn) or expressive (Fire/Leo)?
- Learn to recognize and respect the emotional styles of those close to you.
- Communicate your needs clearly. For example, a Cancer Moon might say, "I need reassurance," while an Aquarius Moon might prefer to handle emotions independently.

Self-Care Aligned with Your Moon Sign

Your Moon sign reveals the best forms of self-care for your unique emotional blueprint. Here are some general tips:

- **Fire Moons**: Prioritize movement and spontaneous fun. Avoid overly rigid routines.
- **Earth Moons**: Focus on physical comfort and tangible achievements. Schedule downtime.
- **Air Moons**: Keep your mind engaged with stimulating books, puzzles, or meaningful conversations.
- **Water Moons**: Embrace solitude and creative outlets. Allow yourself to feel deeply without judgment.

Final Thoughts

Your Moon sign is your emotional compass, guiding you through the highs and lows of life. By understanding its influence, you can better navigate your feelings, manage stress, and nurture meaningful relationships. The Moon's wisdom lies in its quiet presence—always there, reflecting light even in the darkest moments. Let it illuminate your inner world and lead you toward emotional balance and fulfillment.

Chapter 3: Rising Signs and First Impressions

The Rising sign, also known as the Ascendant, is one of the most intriguing and influential aspects of your astrological profile. Often referred to as the "mask" you wear, the Rising sign governs how others perceive you, your outward demeanor, and the first impressions you leave. It's not just about physical appearance—it also reflects your instinctive reactions to the world and the energy you project in new situations.

Understanding your Rising sign can unlock a deeper layer of self-awareness, helping you align your external image with your personal goals and navigate social interactions with confidence.

What Is the Rising (Ascendant) Sign?

The Rising sign is the zodiac sign that was on the eastern horizon at the exact moment of your birth. It changes approximately every two hours, making it highly time-sensitive. While your Sun sign reveals your core self and your Moon sign reflects your emotions, the Rising sign represents your outward expression—how you "show up" in the world.

Think of the Rising sign as your cosmic calling card. It influences:

- **Physical Appearance**: General body language, facial expressions, and even style preferences.
- **First Impressions**: The energy you radiate when meeting others for the first time.
- **Initial Reactions**: Your instinctive approach to new situations, including how you handle introductions and challenges.

While the Rising sign shapes the surface layer of your personality, it's deeply intertwined with the rest of your astrological chart, particularly the planetary alignments in your First House.

How to Determine Your Rising Sign

To identify your Rising sign, you'll need:

1. **Exact Birth Time**: Since the Ascendant shifts approximately every two hours, knowing your precise time of birth is crucial.
2. **Date and Place of Birth**: These details help determine the zodiac sign rising over the horizon at your location.

With this information, you can:

- Use an online Rising sign calculator.
- Refer to a detailed birth chart (natal chart) generated by an astrology app or astrologer.
- Consult astrological software that factors in local time zones and daylight saving adjustments.

If you don't know your exact birth time, your Rising sign may be harder to pinpoint, but an astrologer can help narrow it down based on key personality traits and life events.

The Traits of Each Rising Sign

Below is a snapshot of how each Rising sign influences first impressions, outward appearance, and instinctive reactions.

Fire Signs: Aries, Leo, Sagittarius

- **Aries Rising**: Dynamic, assertive, and energetic. You come across as confident and action-oriented, with an air of leadership.
  Outward Appearance: Athletic build, sharp features, and a brisk pace.
  First Impression Tip: Your directness can be inspiring but soften your approach to avoid overwhelming others.
- **Leo Rising**: Charismatic, warm, and commanding. You exude confidence and a natural flair for attention.
  Outward Appearance: Bold posture, radiant smile, and a preference for stylish or eye-catching outfits.
  First Impression Tip: Balance your charisma with genuine interest in others to foster deeper connections.
- **Sagittarius Rising**: Open-minded, adventurous, and optimistic. You radiate a sense of freedom and curiosity.
  Outward Appearance: Tall or athletic frame, expressive eyes, and a casual, outdoorsy style.
  First Impression Tip: Use your natural enthusiasm to inspire but remain mindful of appearing overly blunt.

Earth Signs: Taurus, Virgo, Capricorn

- **Taurus Rising**: Grounded, calm, and dependable. You give off a sense of stability and warmth.
  Outward Appearance: Strong build, symmetrical features, and a preference for earthy or luxurious fabrics.
  First Impression Tip: Your steady presence is appealing, but try to show flexibility in new situations.
- **Virgo Rising**: Polished, analytical, and helpful. You come across as organized and detail-oriented.
  Outward Appearance: Neat and modest clothing, a refined demeanor, and an observant gaze.
  First Impression Tip: Your focus on precision is admirable—remember to relax and let spontaneity shine through.
- **Capricorn Rising**: Ambitious, composed, and disciplined. You project a sense of professionalism and reliability.
  Outward Appearance: Slim or structured build, sharp cheekbones, and a preference for classic or formal attire.
  First Impression Tip: While your seriousness commands respect, showing a lighter side can help put others at ease.

Air Signs: Gemini, Libra, Aquarius

- **Gemini Rising**: Friendly, quick-witted, and adaptable. You radiate a playful, curious energy.
  Outward Appearance: Youthful appearance, animated gestures, and a knack for expressive conversation.
  First Impression Tip: Your charm is magnetic, but avoid overwhelming others with rapid shifts in focus.
- **Libra Rising**: Graceful, charming, and harmonious. You create a welcoming and aesthetically pleasing presence.
  Outward Appearance: Balanced features, elegant style, and a tendency toward fashionable attire.
  First Impression Tip: While you naturally attract people, assert your preferences to avoid being overly accommodating.
- **Aquarius Rising**: Unique, forward-thinking, and unpredictable. You stand out as innovative and independent.
  Outward Appearance: Distinctive or unconventional features, quirky clothing, and a progressive vibe.
  First Impression Tip: Let your individuality shine while finding common ground to connect with others.

Water Signs: Cancer, Scorpio, Pisces

- **Cancer Rising**: Nurturing, sensitive, and approachable. You project warmth and emotional depth.
  Outward Appearance: Soft features, rounder build, and a preference for comfortable or homey attire.
  First Impression Tip: Your empathy is magnetic, but guard against absorbing too much of others' emotions.
- **Scorpio Rising**: Intense, mysterious, and magnetic. You draw people in with a quiet yet commanding presence.
  Outward Appearance: Piercing eyes, strong jawline, and a preference for darker or dramatic clothing.
  First Impression Tip: Your enigmatic aura is intriguing—balance intensity with openness for stronger bonds.
- **Pisces Rising**: Dreamy, compassionate, and artistic. You exude a sense of imagination and otherworldliness.
  Outward Appearance: Ethereal features, fluid movements, and a love for soft or bohemian styles.
  First Impression Tip: Use your creativity to connect, but stay grounded to avoid seeming aloof.

Aligning Personal Goals with Your Rising Sign Traits

Your Rising sign offers a valuable blueprint for presenting yourself authentically and aligning your goals with the image you project. Here's how to leverage your Ascendant energy:

1. **Enhance Your Strengths**

   Identify the traits associated with your Rising sign and amplify them. For example, a Leo Rising might focus on improving public speaking skills, while a Virgo Rising could refine their organizational abilities.

2. **Balance First Impressions**

   Reflect on how others perceive you. If your Rising sign's traits feel too strong (e.g., Aries Rising's intensity), find ways to balance them, such as practicing active listening or showing vulnerability.

3. **Set Aligned Goals**

   Your Rising sign can inspire goal-setting in areas where you naturally excel. A Sagittarius Rising may pursue travel-related ambitions, while a Taurus Rising might aim for financial stability.

4. **Curate Your Personal Style**

   Use your Rising sign to guide your wardrobe, grooming, and overall aesthetic. Dressing in harmony with your Ascendant's energy can boost your confidence and help you feel authentically "you."

5. **Navigate New Situations**

   In unfamiliar environments, your Rising sign determines your instinctive reactions. Understanding this can help you adapt. For example, a Scorpio Rising might instinctively observe before engaging, while a Gemini Rising might dive into conversations.

Final Thoughts

Your Rising sign is your window to the world—a reflection of how others see you and how you approach new experiences. By understanding its influence, you can refine your outward presentation, enhance first impressions, and align your actions with your deeper goals. Remember, your Rising sign isn't a mask to hide behind—it's a dynamic tool to help you navigate life with authenticity and purpose.

Chapter 4: The Busy Bee's Guide to Planetary Influences

Astrology goes beyond the Sun, Moon, and Rising signs. The planets in our solar system each play a vital role in shaping specific aspects of our lives. While the Sun defines your core identity and the Moon governs your emotions, planets like Mercury, Venus, and Mars are the dynamic forces influencing communication, love, and action. For the busy individual, understanding these planetary influences offers quick insights into how to navigate everyday interactions and challenges.

The Role of Mercury, Venus, and Mars in Astrology

- **Mercury**: The planet of communication, intellect, and thought processes. It governs how we express ourselves, process information, and handle technology.
- **Venus**: The planet of love, beauty, and harmony. It reflects how we experience relationships, our values, and what brings us joy.
- **Mars**: The planet of action, energy, and drive. It dictates how we assert ourselves, pursue goals, and handle conflict.

Together, these planets influence key areas of life, from how you write emails and resolve arguments to how you approach romance and take decisive action.

Quick Interpretations of Planetary Positions
Mercury: Communication and Thought

Mercury's position in your birth chart determines your communication style, decision-making process, and intellectual tendencies.

- **Mercury in Fire Signs (Aries, Leo, Sagittarius)**: Direct, energetic, and enthusiastic. You're a fast thinker and bold communicator but may struggle with patience.
  Practical Application: Use your quick wit to energize conversations, but practice active listening.
- **Mercury in Earth Signs (Taurus, Virgo, Capricorn)**: Practical, methodical, and detail-oriented. You excel at problem-solving and clear articulation but may come across as overly cautious.
  Practical Application: Break complex ideas into actionable steps for yourself and others.
- **Mercury in Air Signs (Gemini, Libra, Aquarius)**: Curious, articulate, and sociable. You're a natural networker but may overthink or scatter your energy.
  Practical Application: Focus on key points in conversations to avoid overwhelming others.
- **Mercury in Water Signs (Cancer, Scorpio, Pisces)**: Intuitive, emotional, and reflective. You communicate with depth and sensitivity but may internalize too much.
  Practical Application: Balance emotional insight with logical clarity to ensure you're understood.

Venus: Love, Beauty, and Values

Venus reveals what you value in relationships, your approach to romance, and your aesthetic preferences.

- **Venus in Fire Signs (Aries, Leo, Sagittarius)**: Passionate, bold, and expressive. You pursue love with enthusiasm but may need to temper impulsiveness.

  Practical Application: Show appreciation through grand gestures but balance them with genuine emotional connection.

- **Venus in Earth Signs (Taurus, Virgo, Capricorn)**: Loyal, grounded, and sensual. You value stability and practical expressions of love but may struggle to express emotions openly.

  Practical Application: Prioritize quality time and tangible acts of care in relationships.

- **Venus in Air Signs (Gemini, Libra, Aquarius)**: Charming, intellectual, and sociable. You thrive on mental stimulation but may avoid emotional intensity.

  Practical Application: Engage in meaningful conversations to deepen emotional bonds.

- **Venus in Water Signs (Cancer, Scorpio, Pisces)**: Romantic, empathetic, and intuitive. You form deep emotional connections but may be prone to moodiness.

  Practical Application: Communicate your emotional needs clearly to avoid misunderstandings.

Mars: Action, Drive, and Passion

Mars governs how you assert yourself, take action, and channel your energy.

- **Mars in Fire Signs (Aries, Leo, Sagittarius)**: Bold, ambitious, and energetic. You're a go-getter but may be prone to burnout or impatience.
  Practical Application: Use your energy to inspire others, but pace yourself for long-term goals.
- **Mars in Earth Signs (Taurus, Virgo, Capricorn)**: Steady, disciplined, and practical. You excel at achieving long-term goals but may struggle with spontaneity.
  Practical Application: Set realistic milestones and celebrate small victories along the way.
- **Mars in Air Signs (Gemini, Libra, Aquarius)**: Strategic, intellectual, and collaborative. You excel in brainstorming but may hesitate to take immediate action.
  Practical Application: Combine your ideas with decisive action for tangible results.
- **Mars in Water Signs (Cancer, Scorpio, Pisces)**: Emotionally driven, intuitive, and persistent. You pursue goals with passion but may take things personally.
  Practical Application: Channel emotional energy into creative or meaningful pursuits.

Recognizing Planetary Retrogrades

A planetary retrograde occurs when a planet appears to move backward in its orbit from our perspective on Earth. While this is an optical illusion, retrogrades have symbolic meanings in astrology. They represent times to slow down, reflect, and reassess the areas of life governed by the retrograde planet.

Mercury Retrograde

- **Effects**: Miscommunication, technology glitches, and delays.
- **What to Do**: Double-check plans, back up important data, and practice patience in conversations.

Venus Retrograde

- **Effects**: Reassessing relationships, shifts in values, and financial reconsiderations.
- **What to Do**: Reflect on what you truly value in love and money. Avoid making major relationship or aesthetic decisions.

Mars Retrograde

- **Effects**: Reduced energy, frustration, and reevaluation of goals.
- **What to Do**: Focus on refining strategies and avoid forcing outcomes. Rest when needed.

Practical Applications of Planetary Influences
In Communication (Mercury)

- Prepare for important conversations by considering your audience's communication style.
- Use Mercury retrograde as an opportunity to review old ideas or rekindle connections.

In Love and Relationships (Venus)

- Align date nights or creative activities with Venusian themes of beauty and connection.
- Use Venus retrograde to heal old wounds and reflect on relationship patterns.

In Action and Career (Mars)

- Harness Mars energy to tackle challenging tasks or start new ventures.
- During Mars retrograde, focus on finishing incomplete projects instead of starting new ones.

Final Thoughts

Mercury, Venus, and Mars are the dynamic trio shaping how you think, love, and act. By understanding their positions in your chart and recognizing their retrograde phases, you can align your actions with cosmic rhythms and navigate life's complexities with greater ease. For the busy individual, these planetary insights are practical tools for achieving more harmony, clarity, and purpose in daily life.

Chapter 5: Astrology in Everyday Life

Astrology isn't just a tool for self-discovery—it's a practical guide for navigating the ebb and flow of daily life. By integrating its wisdom into your routines, decision-making, and relationships, you can unlock insights that enhance your productivity, time management, and connections with others. Best of all, you don't need to spend hours poring over charts; a few simple practices can align your life with the rhythms of the cosmos.

Why Use Astrology in Everyday Life?

Astrology provides a framework for understanding life's patterns and cycles. It helps you:

- Recognize opportunities for growth.
- Prepare for challenges.
- Make decisions that align with your personal energy.
- Strengthen relationships by understanding others' tendencies and communication styles.

Incorporating astrology doesn't require an extensive time investment. By focusing on key elements—like daily transits, Moon phases, and planetary movements—you can seamlessly weave its insights into your everyday life.

Incorporating Astrology into Daily Routines
Morning Rituals with Astrology

- **Daily Transits Check**: Spend 5 minutes reviewing the day's planetary transits. Apps and online resources can provide quick summaries of the energy you can expect. For example:
    - A Moon in Aries day is ideal for tackling bold initiatives.
    - Venus trine Jupiter signals a great day for socializing or creative work.
- **Set Intentions**: Align your goals with the day's astrological energy. If Mercury is in a harmonious aspect, focus on clear communication tasks like emails or presentations.

Midday Energy Boosts

- **Lunchtime Reflections**: Use the current Moon phase to guide your focus:
    - **New Moon**: Reflect on new beginnings and set goals.
    - **Full Moon**: Celebrate accomplishments and evaluate progress.
    - **Waning Moon**: Declutter your mind or space as you prepare for renewal.
- **Astrological Affirmations**: Create affirmations based on your Sun, Moon, or Rising signs. For example, a Capricorn Rising might affirm, "I embrace steady progress and celebrate my discipline."

Evening Wind-Down with the Stars

- **Astrology Journaling**: Write about how the day's energies affected your mood, productivity, or relationships.
- **Plan for Tomorrow**: Check tomorrow's transits and adjust your to-do list to align with the cosmic weather.

Using Astrology for Decision-Making and Time Management

Astrology can guide when and how you tackle important decisions or projects.

Best Timing for Key Activities

- **Mercury and Communication**: Launch projects, sign contracts, or make important announcements when Mercury is direct and well-aspected. Avoid Mercury retrograde for major commitments unless revisiting or refining existing plans.
- **Venus and Relationships**: Plan romantic dates or creative endeavors when Venus is in a favorable position, such as a trine or sextile to Jupiter or Neptune.
- **Mars and Action**: Start new initiatives, fitness routines, or assertive actions during a Mars transit through Fire or Earth signs for enhanced energy and drive.

Aligning with the Moon's Cycle

The Moon's phases and zodiac signs influence your energy and focus. Here's how to use them for time management:

- **New Moon**: Start new projects, set goals, and visualize success.
- **First Quarter Moon**: Take action on your plans and overcome obstacles.
- **Full Moon**: Reflect, celebrate milestones, and focus on relationships.
- **Last Quarter Moon**: Release what no longer serves you and prepare for the next cycle.

Astrology and Daily Scheduling

- Plan mentally demanding tasks during Mercury-ruled days (Wednesday or Gemini/Virgo transits).
- Focus on self-care or emotional tasks during Cancer Moon days.
- Tackle bold, physical tasks during Aries or Leo Moon transits.

Enhancing Relationship Dynamics with Astrology

Astrology offers tools to understand and improve how you interact with others.

Understanding Zodiac Compatibility

While Sun sign compatibility is popular, it's just one piece of the puzzle. Consider these factors:

- **Moon Signs**: Emotional compatibility and how you handle conflicts.
- **Venus Signs**: Romantic and social chemistry.
- **Mars Signs**: Passion and how you handle disagreements.

Practical Relationship Tips

- **Family Dynamics**: If a loved one's Moon sign is in a sensitive Water sign (Cancer, Scorpio, Pisces), approach conflicts with empathy.
- **Workplace Communication**: Adapt your style to colleagues' Mercury signs. For example, a Mercury in Capricorn coworker may prefer concise and professional communication, while a Mercury in Gemini thrives on brainstorming sessions.
- **Romantic Relationships**: Plan dates aligned with your partner's Venus sign preferences. A Taurus Venus might enjoy a cozy dinner, while a Sagittarius Venus may prefer an adventurous outing.

Staying Attuned to Monthly Astrological Transits

Astrological transits are the ongoing movements of planets through the zodiac and their influence on your life.

How to Track Transits

1. **Use an Astrology Calendar**: Many apps and websites provide daily, weekly, and monthly transits.
2. **Focus on Major Transits**: Key events, like a New Moon in your Rising sign's zodiac or Venus entering your Sun sign, often have the most noticeable effects.
3. **Journal Retrogrades**: Note the start and end dates of retrogrades for Mercury, Venus, and Mars, and track how they influence your decisions and emotions.

Practical Tips for Monthly Planning

- **Plan Around the New and Full Moons**: Start projects or intentions at the New Moon and aim to complete milestones by the Full Moon.
- **Note Planetary Shifts**: When planets change signs, the energy of certain areas in your life will shift. For example, when Venus enters Leo, relationships may become more dramatic or expressive.
- **Work With Eclipses**: Solar and Lunar eclipses are powerful times for transformation. Reflect on major themes in your life during these periods.

Final Thoughts

Astrology is a powerful tool for enriching daily life, from aligning your schedule with the Moon's phases to enhancing relationships with zodiac insights. By tuning into the cosmos, you'll develop a deeper sense of flow and purpose, even amidst life's chaos. Whether you have five minutes or an hour, the stars are always there to guide you—use their wisdom to make every day count.

Appendix A: Quick Astrology Glossary

This concise glossary provides definitions of essential astrological terms and symbols, offering quick and accessible guidance for readers at all levels. Use it as a reference to clarify concepts and deepen your understanding of astrology as you explore its applications.

Astrological Terms

Ascendant (Rising Sign)

The zodiac sign rising on the eastern horizon at the time of your birth. It represents your outward personality, first impressions, and instinctive reactions.

Aspects

The angles formed between planets in a birth chart, revealing how they interact. Common aspects include:

- **Conjunction (0°)**: Planets are in the same sign or close together, intensifying their energies.
- **Opposition (180°)**: Planets are directly across from each other, often indicating tension or balance.
- **Trine (120°)**: Planets form a harmonious connection, signifying ease and flow.
- **Square (90°)**: Indicates challenges and opportunities for growth.
- **Sextile (60°)**: A supportive aspect, encouraging opportunities and collaboration.

Birth Chart (Natal Chart)

A map of the sky at the exact time, date, and place of your birth, showing the positions of planets, signs, and houses.

Cardinal Signs

Aries, Cancer, Libra, and Capricorn. These signs are initiators and represent the beginning of each season.

Decan

Each zodiac sign is divided into three 10-degree segments, or decans, adding nuance to astrological interpretations.

Elements

The four fundamental energies that classify zodiac signs:

- **Fire**: Aries, Leo, Sagittarius (passionate and dynamic).
- **Earth**: Taurus, Virgo, Capricorn (practical and grounded).
- **Air**: Gemini, Libra, Aquarius (intellectual and communicative).
- **Water**: Cancer, Scorpio, Pisces (emotional and intuitive).

Ephemeris

A table or online resource showing the daily positions of planets, useful for tracking transits and planning.

Fixed Signs

Taurus, Leo, Scorpio, and Aquarius. These signs are stable, persistent, and associated with the middle of each season.

Houses

The 12 divisions of a birth chart, representing different areas of life (e.g., relationships, career, home). Each house corresponds to a zodiac sign.

Mutable Signs

Gemini, Virgo, Sagittarius, and Pisces. These signs are adaptable and associated with transitions at the end of each season.

Nodes (Lunar Nodes)

Points where the Moon's orbit intersects the ecliptic.

- **North Node**: Represents your soul's purpose and growth.
- **South Node**: Reflects past experiences and habits.

Retrograde

When a planet appears to move backward in the sky from Earth's perspective. Retrogrades are times for reflection and reassessment.

Stellium

Three or more planets in the same zodiac sign or house, intensifying the energy of that sign or area.

Transits

The ongoing movement of planets through the sky and their influence on your birth chart.

Planets and Their Symbols

Personal Planets

Influence daily interactions and individual personality traits.

- ◈ **Sun**: Core identity, vitality, and life purpose.
- ◈ **Moon**: Emotions, intuition, and inner self.
- ◈ **Mercury**: Communication, thought processes, and intellect.
- ♀ **Venus**: Love, beauty, relationships, and values.
- ♂ **Mars**: Action, drive, ambition, and passion.

Social Planets

Shape collective themes and long-term personal development.

- **Jupiter**: Growth, expansion, luck, and wisdom.
- **Saturn**: Discipline, structure, responsibility, and life lessons.

Outer Planets

Influence generational and spiritual transformations.

- **Uranus**: Innovation, rebellion, and change.
- **Neptune**: Dreams, spirituality, and illusions.
- **Pluto**: Transformation, power, and rebirth.

Zodiac Signs and Their Symbols

Each zodiac sign has unique qualities and corresponds to a symbol:

- **Aries**: Bold, pioneering, and action-oriented.
- **Taurus**: Stable, sensual, and persistent.
- **Gemini**: Curious, sociable, and versatile.
- **Cancer**: Nurturing, emotional, and protective.
- **Leo**: Charismatic, creative, and confident.
- **Virgo**: Analytical, detail-oriented, and practical.
- **Libra**: Diplomatic, charming, and fair-minded.
- **Scorpio**: Intense, transformative, and passionate.
- **Sagittarius**: Adventurous, optimistic, and philosophical.
- **Capricorn**: Disciplined, ambitious, and responsible.
- **Aquarius**: Innovative, independent, and visionary.
- **Pisces**: Imaginative, empathetic, and artistic.

Moon Phases and Their Meaning

The Moon phases influence energy and emotions:

- **New Moon**: Beginnings, intention setting.
- **First Quarter Moon**: Action, overcoming obstacles.
- **Full Moon**: Culmination, reflection, and celebration.
- **Last Quarter Moon**: Release, preparation for renewal.

Key Astrological Events

- **Equinox**: Occurs when day and night are equal in length, signaling the start of spring (Aries) or fall (Libra).
- **Solstice**: Marks the longest (Cancer) and shortest (Capricorn) days of the year.
- **Eclipses**: Solar or lunar, these events amplify change and transformation.

Astrological Symbols for Aspects

- ☌ **Conjunction**: Planets together, amplifying energy.
- ⚹ **Sextile**: Cooperative and productive energy.
- □ **Square**: Tension and challenges.
- △ **Trine**: Harmony and ease.
- ☍ **Opposition**: Balance or conflict between energies.

This glossary is your go-to reference for understanding astrology's foundational concepts and symbols. Keep it handy as you delve deeper into the cosmic wisdom guiding your life.

Appendix B: Star Sign Cheat Sheets

This appendix provides printable summaries of Sun, Moon, and Rising sign traits for all 12 zodiac signs, offering quick reference to each sign's key characteristics. Additionally, a simple chart is included to help track your personal planetary placements, making it easy to integrate astrology into your daily life.

Star Sign Cheat Sheets: Sun, Moon, and Rising Traits

Aries (March 21 – April 19)

- **Sun Traits**: Energetic, confident, bold, and competitive. A natural leader who thrives on challenges.
- **Moon Traits**: Emotionally intense, quick to react, and fiercely independent. Needs excitement and purpose to feel secure.
- **Rising Traits**: Dynamic and enthusiastic. Leaves a strong first impression of confidence and drive.

Taurus (April 20 – May 20)

- **Sun Traits**: Practical, patient, loyal, and grounded. Values stability, comfort, and beauty.
- **Moon Traits**: Emotionally steady, sensual, and nurturing. Needs security and physical comfort for peace of mind.
- **Rising Traits**: Calm, reliable, and approachable. Projects an aura of stability and warmth.

Gemini (May 21 – June 20)

- **Sun Traits**: Curious, adaptable, witty, and sociable. Enjoys variety and mental stimulation.
- **Moon Traits**: Emotionally versatile, communicative, and easily bored. Needs intellectual engagement to feel fulfilled.
- **Rising Traits**: Quick-witted and charming. Leaves a lively and approachable first impression.

Cancer (June 21 – July 22)

- **Sun Traits**: Nurturing, sensitive, intuitive, and protective. Deeply connected to family and home.
- **Moon Traits**: Emotionally intense, empathetic, and sentimental. Needs emotional security and close connections.
- **Rising Traits**: Warm and caring. Projects a nurturing and approachable energy.

Leo (July 23 – August 22)

- **Sun Traits**: Confident, creative, generous, and charismatic. Thrives on recognition and self-expression.
- **Moon Traits**: Emotionally expressive, loyal, and dramatic. Needs affection and validation to feel secure.
- **Rising Traits**: Radiant and magnetic. Leaves a bold, confident, and creative impression.

Virgo (August 23 – September 22)

- **Sun Traits**: Analytical, practical, detail-oriented, and service-driven. Strives for perfection and efficiency.
- **Moon Traits**: Emotionally grounded, cautious, and thoughtful. Needs routine and order for emotional balance.
- **Rising Traits**: Polished and composed. Projects an organized, intelligent, and capable demeanor.

Libra (September 23 – October 22)

- **Sun Traits**: Diplomatic, charming, fair-minded, and harmonious. Values relationships and aesthetic beauty.
- **Moon Traits**: Emotionally balanced, social, and relationship-focused. Needs harmony and connection to feel secure.
- **Rising Traits**: Graceful and charming. Leaves a friendly and sophisticated impression.

Scorpio (October 23 – November 21)

- **Sun Traits**: Intense, passionate, resourceful, and transformative. Thrives on depth and uncovering truths.
- **Moon Traits**: Emotionally deep, private, and intuitive. Needs emotional intensity and authenticity to feel fulfilled.
- **Rising Traits**: Mysterious and magnetic. Projects a powerful and transformative energy.

Sagittarius (November 22 – December 21)

- **Sun Traits**: Optimistic, adventurous, independent, and philosophical. Values freedom and exploration.
- **Moon Traits**: Emotionally free-spirited, enthusiastic, and restless. Needs adventure and meaning for emotional security.

- **Rising Traits**: Open and friendly. Projects an adventurous and optimistic vibe.

Capricorn (December 22 – January 19)

- **Sun Traits**: Ambitious, disciplined, practical, and responsible. Focused on long-term success.
- **Moon Traits**: Emotionally reserved, patient, and pragmatic. Needs structure and accomplishment to feel secure.
- **Rising Traits**: Serious and professional. Leaves an impression of reliability and ambition.

Aquarius (January 20 – February 18)

- **Sun Traits**: Innovative, independent, visionary, and unconventional. Thrives on originality and progressive thinking.
- **Moon Traits**: Emotionally detached, intellectual, and idealistic. Needs freedom and mental stimulation for balance.
- **Rising Traits**: Unique and forward-thinking. Projects an innovative and independent energy.

Pisces (February 19 – March 20)

- **Sun Traits**: Compassionate, imaginative, intuitive, and artistic. Deeply connected to emotions and spirituality.
- **Moon Traits**: Emotionally empathetic, dreamy, and sensitive. Needs creative outlets and emotional connection to feel secure.
- **Rising Traits**: Gentle and ethereal. Projects a compassionate and mystical aura.

Personal Planetary Placements Tracking Chart

Use this chart to document your Sun, Moon, Rising, and planetary placements for easy reference.

Planet/Aspect	Sign	Key Traits
☉ Sun	(e.g., Leo)	Core identity, vitality, life purpose
☽ Moon	(e.g., Cancer)	Emotions, intuition, inner self
Ascendant (Rising)	(e.g., Virgo)	First impressions, outward personality
☿ Mercury	(e.g., Gemini)	Communication, thought processes, intellect
♀ Venus	(e.g., Taurus)	Love, beauty, relationships, values
♂ Mars	(e.g., Aries)	Action, energy, ambition, passion
♃ Jupiter	(e.g., Sagittarius)	Growth, luck, wisdom
♄ Saturn	(e.g., Capricorn)	Discipline, responsibility, life lessons
♅ Uranus	(e.g., Aquarius)	Innovation, rebellion, change

Planet/Aspect	Sign	Key Traits
◈ **Neptune**	(e.g., Pisces)	Dreams, spirituality, imagination
◈ **Pluto**	(e.g., Scorpio)	Transformation, power, rebirth
North Node	(e.g., Gemini)	Soul purpose, life direction
South Node	(e.g., Sagittarius)	Past habits, experiences

This cheat sheet and chart are designed to simplify your astrological journey, making it easy to track and interpret key influences in your life. Print this appendix for quick reference and take your first step toward mastering the stars!

<u>Message from the Author:</u>

I hope you enjoyed this book, I love astrology and knew there was not a book such as this out on the shelf. I love metaphysical items as well. Please check out my other books:

-Life of Government Benefits

-My life of Hell

-My life with Hydrocephalus

-Red Sky

-World Domination:Woman's rule

-World Domination:Woman's Rule 2: The War

-Life and Banishment of Apophis: book 1

-The Kidney Friendly Diet

-The Ultimate Hemp Cookbook

-Creating a Dispensary(legally)

-Cleanliness throughout life: the importance of showering from childhood to adulthood.

-Strong Roots: The Risks of Overcoddling children

-Hemp Horoscopes: Cosmic Insights and Earthly Healing

- Celestial Hemp Navigating the Zodiac: Through the Green Cosmos

-Astrological Hemp: Aligning The Stars with Earth's Ancient Herb

-The Astrological Guide to Hemp: Stars, Signs, and Sacred Leaves

-Green Growth: Innovative Marketing Strategies for your Hemp Products and Dispensary

-Cosmic Cannabis

-Astrological Munchies

-Henry The Hemp

-Zodiacal Roots: The Astrological Soul Of Hemp

- **Green Constellations: Intersection of Hemp and Zodiac**

-Hemp in The Houses: An astrological Adventure Through The Cannabis Galaxy

-Galactic Ganja Guide

Heavenly Hemp
Zodiac Leaves
Doctor Who Astrology
Cannastrology
Stellar Satvias and Cosmic Indicas
<u>Celestial Cannabis: A Zodiac Journey</u>
AstroHerbology: The Sky and The Soil: Volume 1
AstroHerbology:Celestial Cannabis:Volume 2
Cosmic Cannabis Cultivation
The Starry Guide to Herbal Harmony: Volume 1
The Starry Guide to Herbal Harmony: Cannabis Universe: Volume 2

Yugioh Astrology: Astrological Guide to Deck, Duels and more
Nightmare Mansion: Echoes of The Abyss
Nightmare Mansion 2: Legacy of Shadows
Nightmare Mansion 3: Shadows of the Forgotten
Nightmare Mansion 4: Echoes of the Damned
The Life and Banishment of Apophis: Book 2
Nightmare Mansion: Halls of Despair
<u>Healing with Herb: Cannabis and Hydrocephalus</u>
<u>Planetary Pot: Aligning with Astrological Herbs: Volume 1</u>
Fast Track to Freedom: 30 Days to Financial Independence Using AI, Assets, and Agile Hustles
<u>Cosmic Hemp Pathways</u>
How to Become Financially Free in 30 Days: 10,000 Paths to Prosperity
Zodiacal Herbage: Astrological Insights: Volume 1
Nightmare Mansion: Whispers in the Walls
The Daleks Invade Atlantis
Henry the hemp and Hydrocephalus

10X The Kidney Friendly Diet
Cannabis Universe: Adult coloring book

Hemp Astrology: The Healing Power of the Stars

Zodiacal Herbage: Astrological Insights: Cannabis Universe: Volume 2

<u>**Planetary Pot: Aligning with Astrological Herbs: Cannabis Universes: Volume 2**</u>

Doctor Who Meets the Replicators and SG-1: The Ultimate Battle for Survival

Nightmare Mansion: Curse of the Blood Moon

<u>**The Celestial Stoner: A Guide to the Zodiac**</u>

Cosmic Pleasures: Sex Toy Astrology for Every Sign

Hydrocephalus Astrology: Navigating the Stars and Healing Waters

Lapis and the Mischievous Chocolate Bar

Celestial Positions: Sexual Astrology for Every Sign

Apophis's Shadow Work Journal: : A Journey of Self-Discovery and Healing

Kinky Cosmos: Sexual Kink Astrology for Every Sign

Digital Cosmos: The Astrological Digimon Compendium

Stellar Seeds: The Cosmic Guide to Growing with Astrology

Apophis's Daily Gratitude Journal

Cat Astrology: Feline Mysteries of the Cosmos

The Cosmic Kama Sutra: An Astrological Guide to Sexual Positions

Unleash Your Potential: A Guided Journal Powered by AI Insights

Whispers of the Enchanted Grove

Cosmic Pleasures: An Astrological Guide to Sexual Kinks

369, 12 Manifestation Journal

Whisper of the nocturne journal(blank journal for writing or drawing)

The Boogey Book

Locked In Reflection: A Chastity Journey Through Locktober

Generating Wealth Quickly:

How to Generate $100,000 in 24 Hours

Star Magic: Harness the Power of the Universe

The Flatulence Chronicles: A Fart Journal for Self-Discovery

The Doctor and The Death Moth

Seize the Day: A Personal Seizure Tracking Journal

The Ultimate Boogeyman Safari: A Journey into the Boogie World and Beyond

Whispers of Samhain: 1,000 Spells of Love, Luck, and Lunar Magic: Samhain Spell Book

Apophis's guides:

Witch's Spellbook Crafting Guide for Halloween

<u>Frost & Flame: The Enchanted Yule Grimoire of 1000 Winter Spells</u>

<u>The Ultimate Boogey Goo Guide & Spooky Activities for Halloween Fun</u>

Harmony of the Scales: A Libra's Spellcraft for Balance and Beauty

The Enchanted Advent: 36 Days of Christmas Wonders

Nightmare Mansion: The Labyrinth of Screams

Harvest of Enchantment: 1,000 Spells of Gratitude, Love, and Fortune for Thanksgiving

The Boogey Chronicles: A Journal of Nightly Encounters and Shadowy Secrets

The 12 Days of Financial Freedom: A Step-by-Step Christmas Countdown to Transform Your Finances

Sigil of the Eternal Spiral Blank Journal

A Christmas Feast: Timeless Recipes for Every Meal

Holiday Stress-Free Solutions: A Survival Guide to Thriving During the Festive Season

Yu-Gi-Oh! Holiday Gifting Mastery: The Ultimate Guide for Fans and Newcomers Alike

Holiday Harmony: A Hydrocephalus Survival Guide for the Festive Season

Celestial Craft: The Witch's Almanac for 2025 – A Cosmic Guide to Manifestations, Moons, and Mystical Events

Doctor Who: The Toymaker's Winter Wonderland

Tulsa King Unveiled: A Thrilling Guide to Stallone's Mafia Masterpiece

Pendulum Craft: A Complete Guide to Crafting and Using Personalized Divination Tools

Nightmare Mansion: Santa's Eternal Eve

Starlight Noel: A Cosmic Journey through Christmas Mysteries

The Dark Architect: Unlocking the Blueprint of Existence

Surviving the Embrace: The Ultimate Guide to Encounters with The Hugging Molly

The Enchanted Codex: Secrets of the Craft for Witches, Wiccans, and Pagans

Harvest of Gratitude: A Complete Thanksgiving Guide

Yuletide Essentials: A Complete Guide to an Authentic and Magical Christmas

Celestial Smokes: A Cosmic Guide to Cigars and Astrology

Living in Balance: A Comprehensive Survival Guide to Thriving with Diabetes Insipidus

Cosmic Symbiosis: The Venom Zodiac Chronicles

The Cursed Paw of Ambition

Cosmic Symbiosis: The Astrological Venom Journal

Celestial Wonders Unfold: A Stargazer's Guide to the Cosmos (2024-2029)

The Ultimate Black Friday Prepper's Guide: Mastering Shopping Strategies and Savings

Cosmic Sales: The Astrological Guide to Black Friday Shopping

Legends of the Corn Mother and Other Harvest Myths

Candy Cane Conjurations
Cooking with Kids: Recipes Under 20 Minutes
Doctor Who: The TARDIS Confiscation
The Anxiety First Aid Kit: Quick Tools to Calm Your Mind
Frosty Whispers: A Winter's Tale
The Infinite Key: Unlocking the Secrets to Prosperity, Resilience, and Purpose
The Grasping Void: Why You'll Regret This Purchase

If you want solar for your home go here: https://www.harborsolar.live/apophisenterprises/

Get Some Tarot cards: https://www.makeplayingcards.com/sell/apophis-occult-shop

Get some shirts: https://www.bonfire.com/store/apophis-shirt-emporium/

<u>Instagrams:</u>
@apophis_enterprises,
@apophisbookemporium,
@apophisscardshop
Twitter: @apophisenterpr1
 Tiktok:@apophisenterprise
Youtube: @sg1fan23477, @FiresideRetreatKingdom
Hive: @sg1fan23477
CheeLee: @SG1fan23477

Podcast: Apophis Chat Zone: https://open.spotify.com/show/5zXbrCLEV2xzCp8ybrfHsk?si=fb4d4fdbdce44dec

Newsletter: https://apophiss-newsletter-27c897.beehiiv.com/

If you want to support me or see posts of other projects that I have come over to: **<u>buymeacoffee.com/mpetchinskg</u>**
I post there daily several times a day

Get your Dinowicca or Christmas themed digital products, especially Santa Raptor songs and other musics. Here:
https://sg1fan23477.gumroad.com

Apophis Yuletide Digital has not only digital Christmas items, but it will have all things with Dinowicca as well as other Digital products.